Praise for

"I've sat in those elder meetings and wondered, How are we supposed to know what to do in this situation? In those cases we've looked to help from our friends in the Sojourn Network, whose experience, wisdom, zeal for the gospel, and love for the Lord has been a great encouragement. I'm thankful for this series because I know how many pastors and other church leaders will benefit from such biblically informed guidance on a host of topics."

Collin Hansen, editorial director, The Gospel Coalition

"Dave Harvey gives us another fantastic book. *Healthy Plurality = Durable Church* is an enjoyable read, very biblical, and memorable. The fact that it is short and a quick read makes it all the more useful."

Matt Perman, author of *What's Best Next: How the Gospel Transforms the Way You Get Things Done*

"Dave Harvey has done a great service for all who love the local church and have been called by God into leadership. He carefully explains why God calls local churches to be overseen by a plurality of leaders. And he steers us around the reefs and barriers that have left some church boards shipwrecked and their churches torn in pieces. By God's grace, healthy plurality in leadership is not only possible - it can be glorious!"

Bob Lepine, Teaching Pastor, Redeemer Community Church, Little Rock AR, Co-Host, FamilyLife Today

"You were never intended to lead your church alone. God's design for the church has always been a plurality of elders—but, even though plurality is right, that doesn't mean plurality is easy. Dave Harvey knows this, and he has provided this short and straightforward guide to help you as a pastor to cultivate the practice of effective plurality in leadership."

> **Timothy Paul Jones**, Ph.D., Associate Vice President, The Southern Baptist Theological Seminary; elder, Sojourn Community Church, Midtown; author of *The God Who Goes Before You: Pastoral Leadership as Christ-Centered Followership*

"It is one thing to believe in the necessity of a plurality of elders but quite another to understand what it actually means! Dave Harvey does an excellent job at explaining it. He put words on reality I have lived for years and wanted to encourage fellow pastors as the dean of my church-based seminary. He describes the type of fellowship that should exist between a team of elders. More than that he sheds more light on our path as a team of elders. I thank God for this precious brother."

> **François Turcotte**, Directeur Général, Séminaire Baptiste Évangélique du Québec (SEMBEC)

z

"Being a pastor/elder of a local church is no small task, and yet many times I wonder if I'm doing it right, especially when working with other elders. That's why I've found Dave Harvey's *Healthy Plurality = Durable Church* so helpful. With a compelling vision and clear manner, Harvey makes the practice of developing a healthy plurality of elders not just understandable, but desirable. If you are planting or leading a local church and you want to see a healthy church exist far beyond your leadership pick up and implement this book in your ministry. It may be the most humbling thing you will ever do, but it will also be the strongest way you will ever lead."

Jeremy Writebol, Lead Campus Pastor, Woodside Bible Church, Plymouth MI

"This brief primer on plurality will be of great help to any church eldership seeking to lead and care well for the people entrusted to them. Dave Harvey has zeroed in on the key principles and has put very useful feet to them. As soon as I read it, this became the book we will discuss on our next elder's retreat and I am sure it will serve our eldering through our deliberations in the years ahead."

Mike Bullmore, Senior Pastor of CrossWay Community Church, Bristol, Wisconsin

"A literary critic once complained of a book, 'Its covers are too far apart.' He was not reviewing *Healthy Plurality*. A page of Dave Harvey offers more hard-lessons-learned, easy-to-miss biblical insight than most six-week sermon series. I rarely leave a conversation with Dave as clueless as I entered it — and this book, especially, packs in multiple such conversations."

> **Steve Estes**, Senior Pastor of Community Evangelical Free Church, Elverson, Pennsylvania; author of several books

Praise for the "How-To" Series

"The Sojourn Network 'How-To' books are a great combination of biblical theology and practical advice, driven by a commitment to the gospel and the local congregation. Written by the local church for the local church — just the job!"

> **Tim Chester**, pastor of Grace Church Boroughbridge, faculty member of Crosslands Training, and author of over 40 books

"This series brings pastoral wisdom for everyday life in the church of Jesus Christ. Think of these short, practical books as the equivalent of a healthy breakfast, a sandwich and apple for lunch, and a family enjoying dinner together. The foundational theology is nutritious, and the practical applications will keep the body strong."

> **Dr. David Powlison**, Executive Director of CCEF; senior editor, Journal of Biblical Counseling; author of *Good and Angry: Redeeming Anger* and *Making All Things New: Restoring Joy to the Sexually Broken*

"Most leaders don't need another abstract book on leadership; we need help with the 'how-to's.' And my friends in the Sojourn Network excel in this area. I've been well served by their practical ministry wisdom, and I know you will be too."

> **Bob Thune**, Founding Pastor, Coram Deo Church, Omaha, NE, author of *Gospel Eldership* and co-author of *The Gospel-Centered Life*

"I cannot express strong enough what a valuable resource this is for church planters, church planting teams and young churches. The topics that are addressed in these books are so needed in young churches. I have been in ministry and missions for over 30 years and I learned a lot from reading. Very engaging and very practical!"

> **Larry McCrary**, Co-Founder and Director of The Upstream Collective

"There are many aspects of pastoral ministry that aren't (and simply can't) be taught in seminary. Even further, many pastors simply don't have the benefit of a brotherhood of pastors that they can lean on to help them navigate topics such as building a healthy plurality of elders or working with artists in the church. I'm thankful for the men and women who labored to produce this series, which is both theologically-driven and practically-minded. The Sojourn Network "How-To" series is a great resource for pastors and church planters alike."

> **Jamaal Williams**, Lead Pastor of Sojourn Midtown, Louisville, KY

"HOW-TO" BUILD AND MAINTAIN A
HEALTHY PLURALITY OF ELDERS

Dave Harvey

Healthy Plurality = Durable Church
"How-To" Build and Maintain a Healthy Plurality of Elders

© 2018 Dave Harvey
All rights reserved.

A publication of Sojourn Network Press in Louisville, KY. For more books by Sojourn Network, visit us at sojournnetwork.com/store.

Cover design: Josh Noom & Benjamin Vrbicek
Interior design: Benjamin Vrbicek

Trade paperback ISBN: 978-1732055209

The Sojourn Network book series is dedicated to the pastors, elders, and deacons of Sojourn Network churches. Because you are faithful, the church will be served and sent as we plant, grow, and multiply healthy churches that last.

CONTENTS

SERIES PREFACE

Why should the Sojourn Network publish a "How-To" series?

It's an excellent question, since it leads to a more personal and pertinent question for you: *Why should you bother to read any of these books?*

Sojourn Network, the ministry I am honored to lead, exists to plant, grow, and multiply healthy networks, churches, and pastors. Therefore, it seems only natural to convert some of our leader's best thinking and practices into written material focusing on the "How-To" aspects of local church ministry and multiplication.

We love church planters and church planting. But we've come to believe it's not enough to do assessments and fund church plants. We must also help, equip, and learn from one another in order to be good shepherds and leaders. We must stir up one another to the good work of leading churches towards their most fruitful future.

That's why some books will lend themselves to soul calibration for ministry longevity, while others will examine the riggings of specific ministries or specialized mission. This is essential work to building ministries *that last*. But God has also placed it on our hearts to share our mistakes and most fruitful practices so that others might improve upon what we have done. This way, everyone wins.

If our prayer is answered, this series will bring thoughtful, pastoral, charitable, gospel-saturated, church-grounded, renewal-based "practice" to the rhythms of local church life and network collaboration.

May these "How-To" guides truly serve you. May they arm you with new ideas for greater leadership effectiveness. Finally, may they inspire you to love Jesus more and serve his people with grace-inspired gladness, in a ministry that passes the test of time.

Dave Harvey
President, Sojourn Network

INTRODUCTORY LETTER

Friends,

When I was in seminary, I occasionally "spaced out" in class. Once during a preaching class, while my mind slipped skyward, a pithy statement from my professor yanked me back to earth. "The best preachers," he said, "will tell folks what he's going to tell them; then he tells them; and then tells them what he told them." "Wow!" I thought. If repetition made for good preaching, then parenting had already given me a serious head start. With four kids, redundancy was like a second language to me. To preach I just needed to take my gift for repetition and drop the 'parental threat' — you know, that final line where you tell them what you would do if they didn't listen. Preaching was going to be simple.

It wasn't. But over time I learned that my professor was essentially right. Redundancy serves folks when you have important things to say. I hope it works for writing too. Because in the very next sentence, I'm going to tell you what I want to tell you, so we can talk about it, and then I can remind you of what we discussed. *Leaders, the quality of your elder plurality determines the health of your church.*

All over the country the fat is hitting the church fire because the principle of plurality is misunderstood or ignored. Do you see it happening? In churches large and small, plurality failures land like a dull axe, brutally splintering many a congregation. Lift the lid of most pastoral failures and the stench of some plurality dysfunction wafts over the senses. Plurality ambiguities or avoidances cast a darkness that incubates some pretty ugly stuff. Dissect the ecosystem of many celebrity-pastor problems and you'll find plurality failures — or worse, no plurality at all.

The quality of your plurality determines the health of your church.

Make no mistake: This saying is trustworthy and worth repeating. *The quality of your plurality determines the health of your church.*

But healthy plurality is hard work. It's part art, part science, and wholly service fused together by men applying tenacious initiative and patient love. Effective pluralities require hearts filled with integrity and wise, skillful hands (Psalm 78:72). And time, lots and lots of time.

My first pastorate lasted 27 years in the same church. For most of that time, I was the lead pastor and we continually tuned and re-tuned our understanding of plurality until it served the church well. We made plenty of mistakes and it was painstakingly hard work. It meant having men get to know me down to the level of my dreams, desires, giftings, and temptations. But I treasure those memories and the fruit that the plurality bore in my life and in the life of our church. Since then I've served on multiple teams in different roles. Sometimes we've applied plurality well; sometimes we've made some big mistakes. But through it all I've only become more convinced of my earlier point: *The quality of your plurality determines the health of your church.*

In this book I will share what I have learned about how to define and assess a healthy plurality of elders, and I hope it is of help to you. We'll look at what makes pluralities durable and what makes them so unpredictably delicate. We'll talk specifically about why and how a healthy plurality contributes to a healthy church, including:

- How healthy pluralities create a context for elder care.
- How healthy pluralities offer authentic community characterized by vulnerability, honesty and growth through self-disclosure.
- How healthy pluralities, and the unity they enjoy, become a microcosm for the entire church.

Plurality matters. Plurality is like character, sooner or later character trumps skill and will determine the health and vitality of the church. So we'll also learn not to assume the health of our unity, but to ask questions that will diagnose the strength and substance of our plurality. Together we will examine:

- Agreement: *do we agree with each other?*
- Trust: *do we trust one another?*
- Care: *do we care for each other?*

- Fit: *do we enjoy being with each other and know where we fit?*

My friends, we're not merely looking for a few laughs, some decent conferences and a few good years together. We want churches that last. But to achieve that goal, we need strong pluralities. Sojourn Network, or any network, will be a success to the extent that we help build strong pluralities. And in the event you're still asking 'why,' permit me the indulgence of another repetition: *Because the quality of our plurality determines the health of the church.*

For the gospel at work in churches that last,
Dave

PHILOSOPHY

A PLURALITY PRIMER

It happened again. Another phone call, another crisis, another pastor walking alone. My heart aches for this guy — leadership for him has always been a lonely experience dependent solely upon his gifts. I hope he sees the different path for leadership that we discussed; the one that goes all the way to God's design.

Human beings are created for community.[1] We are made in the image of the Triune God who dwells in the delights of eternal community.[2] We are relational creatures deriving our existence, salvation, identity and hope from a relational

---

[1] Romans 12:4–5; Hebrews 10:24–25.

[2] The Bible speaks from Genesis to Revelation indicating there is one God who exists in three persons interacting in eternity past with role and relationship within himself, thus the eternal community highlighted in the Genesis creation account (Genesis 1–2) and John 1:1–18 especially, along with the telling words of Christ in John 14 among his many references to the Father and Spirit's closeness and the final Trinitarian formula in Matthew 28:19.

Creator.[3] As God exists in community, we are made to exist in community. This remarkable reality of community shapes what it means to be truly human. The theme of community flows across Scripture and informs church leadership.

Leaders are called to community, connection, and collaboration. And thus we arrive at the idea of "plurality."[4]

The term "plurality" simply reflects the scriptural evidence that New Testament churches were led by more than one leader.[5] The elders,[6] and deacons of the New

> **Leaders are called to community, connection, and collaboration.**

Testament labored together as partners on a team, and enjoyed "plurality" in community that enhanced both decision-making and their respective roles. Plurality means the church is led by a team and through a team. This experience of collaborative-based leadership forms the strength, unity, and integrity of the local church's leadership for durable mission and care.

---

[3] On mankind in God's image: Genesis 1:26–27; 5:1–2; 9:6; James 3:9.

[4] "The apostolic churches seem, in general, to have had a plurality of elders as well as deacons." J.L. Reynolds, "Church Polity or The Kingdom of Christ its Internal and External Development." In *Polity: Biblical Arguments on How to Conduct Church Life (A Collection of Historic Baptist Documents)*, ed. Mark Dever, (Washington, DC: Center for Church Reform, 2001), 349.

[5] "On the local church level, the New Testament plainly witnesses to a consistent pattern of shared pastoral leadership. Therefore, leadership by a plurality of elders is a sound biblical practice." Alexander Strauch, *Biblical Eldership: An Urgent Call to Restore Biblical Church Leadership* (Littleton: Lewis and Roth, 1995), 37.

[6] For a detailed discussion of the Greek words related to the office of elder, see Appendix One.

But why advocate plurality? As we study Scripture, we can offer at least seven reasons why plurality is a foundational leadership model for the local church:

1. Plurality reflects the co-equality, unity and community expressed by the Trinity. (2 Corinthians 13:14; Ephesians 4:4–6; Jude 20–21; 1 Peter 1:2).

2. Plurality was a prominent and essential feature of New Testament church polity.[7]

3. Plurality embodies and expresses the New Testament principle of interdependence and the diversity of gifts among members of Christ's body (Romans 12:4–6; 1 Corinthians 12).

4. Plurality acknowledges human limitations by recognizing that no one elder can possess the full complement of gifts God intends to use, bless, and build the church (1 Corinthians 12:21). For instance, the practice of plurality discourages narcissistic personalities who look to exercise unique and exclusive authority or control within a team. This practice also calls forward timid leaders to shoulder the weight of governing responsibility. Where plurality truly exists, pastors remain appropriately engaged, loved, guided, harnessed, and accountable.

5. Plurality creates a leadership structure where men must model the unity characterizing the church

---

[7] For a detailed discussion of how New Testament elders functioned in plurality, see Appendix One.

(John 17:23; Romans 15:5; Ephesians 4:3, 13; Colossians 3:14).

6. Plurality creates a community of care, calling, support, and accountability for the life and doctrine of the leaders (1 Timothy 4:14, 16; Titus 1:6; James 5:16).

7. Plurality contradicts the idea of "singular genius" and replaces it with a "multitude of counselors" (Proverbs 15:22; 24:6) who collaborate lead and guide the church together. This isn't simply a clever constitutional maneuver, but the recognition that the New Testament pattern assumed that the authority for the local church was given to the entire eldership, not just to one gifted leader. In other words, the responsibility inheres in the group, not the man.[8]

Just to be clear: Advocating the view that God assigns responsibility to a group of leaders is hardly a pioneering approach to church polity. Our Reformed forefathers practiced this polity years ago.[9] Louis Berkhof suggested it is

---

[8] "Today, whatever form of church government a church may have, the officers who have the highest governing authority in the local church (whether they are called elders, pastors, deacons, the vestry, the church board, the governing council, or any other name) are the ones who most closely correspond to the office of elder at the time of the New Testament. They do in fact have governing authority (of varying degrees) in their churches." John Piper, *Recovering Biblical Manhood and Womanhood: A Response to Evangelical Feminism*, ed. John Piper and Wayne Grudem (Wheaton: Crossway, 2006), 256.

[9] "And as the whole spiritual government of each church is committed to its bench of elders, the session is competent to regulate every concern,

precisely the Reformed practice of co-equality among elders that distinguishes their polity from other groups.

> Reformed churches differ, on the one hand, from all those churches in which the government is in the hands of a single prelate or presiding elder, and on the other hand, from those in which it rests with the people in general. They do not believe in any one-man rule, be he an elder, a pastor, or a bishop; neither do they believe in popular government. They choose ruling elders as their representatives, and these, together with the minister(s), form a council or consistory for the government of the local church.[10]

To summarize this point with a quote from a familiar voice in the world of polity, Alexander Strauch says, "Jesus Christ gave the church a plurality of leadership."[11]

A Personal Path

I would love to tell you that I came to these convictions by studying Scripture, analyzing healthy church models, and examining what's been most effective in the history of the church. Actually, though, my convictions have come more from a spiritual slap, if you believe in such things. The

---

and to correct everything which they consider amiss in the arrangements or affairs of the church which admits of correction." Samuel Miller, *An Essay on the Warrant, Nature, and Duties of the Office of the Ruling Elder,* (Philadelphia: Presbyterian Board of Publishing, 1832), 201.

[10] Louis Berkhof, *Summary of Christian Doctrine,* (Grand Rapids: Wm. B. Eerdmans, 1938), 589.

[11] Strauch, *Biblical Eldership*, 36.

moment was a kind of a holy headlock that graciously grabbed me in a defining moment; a kind of a holy headlock where the Spirit graciously grabbed me in my sinfulness and pointed me in a different direction.

Let me tell you about it.

Years ago my wife Kimm and I joined a new church plant in the Philadelphia area. The church grew rapidly from the beginning and within a year, I was invited on staff to help with evangelism, singles ministry, administration, and well, you know, anything else needing to be done. Within a few years some issues surfaced in the life of the lead pastor, which raised questions about whether it was a good role for him. Through a long and difficult process, it became clear he was probably not the guy to lead the church.

This drama raised the question, "Who then should lead the church?"

There was another man on staff who was a lovable, pastoral, fatherly guy who helped start the church. During the church drama, he quickly became the center of care and community. He was a respected voice and he possessed the love and trust of the people. As I look back, it seems like a logic-screaming no-brainer that he should have been the guy to lead, at least until the church stabilized enough to think about the future. He was 13 years older and far more experienced than me. But rather than humbly advocating for him to lead, I resisted his appointment because of certain weaknesses I saw in him. Looking back, I can now admit I had what the world might call a "remarkably high self-esteem," which in Bible-speak means "a prideful, exaggerated assessment of myself." I secretly believed I was better suited for the role. I was perturbed this wasn't obvious to others! Pretty ugly, huh? Even as I type these words three decades later, I still feel the flesh-piercing stab of shame. Thank God for the gospel and the forgiveness of friends.

I'd become jealous and selfishly ambitious. The reality of my blindness was weighty, but my condition made me think my sight was sharper and more discerning. I was too caught up in relational and organizational disorder. Reality had become distorted and exaggerated. This resulted in much talking, but little clarity. Maybe reading about this has you instantly nodding, because you have lived through it yourself. You had a "Dave," or maybe YOU were Dave. If so hang in there, I'm moving towards a defining moment.

For my part, I think what was happening in my heart is described well in James 3:16: "For where jealousy and selfish ambition exist, there will be disorder and every vile practice." Think about it. I had an opportunity to serve a guy more experienced than myself and trusted throughout the church endowed with pastoral gifts. But to my shame, I questioned his leadership and the wisdom of his appointment. Pride and ambition can be evil. Their divisiveness is in

> **Where there is an absence of plurality, jealousy and selfish ambition can easily confuse and corrupt.**

the details. Where there is an absence of plurality, jealousy and selfish ambition can easily confuse and corrupt. My pride was exceptional at confusing and corrupting me.

Little did I know this vital lesson was playing out in a way that profoundly shaped my future. The experience of plurality — leading with another guy through a difficult situation — revealed my heart. If you're new to this whole plurality thing, you'll soon see how often plurality uncovers and forces you to deal with the heroic dreams and fleshly desires you have for ministry. When you think about it, this makes sense. I mean wrapped up in plurality is roles and leadership, coming under authority, learning humility, and a willingness to think about our gifts and position through what serves the church, instead of our own agendas. Leading in community draws us under a holy spotlight inevitably exposing our false identities, a high opinion of our gifts, and our ungodly ambitions.

Thankfully all of my junk came spilling out in a moment in my friend's office. We were once again arguing over something totally irrelevant and unnecessary. But at one point in this conversation, my friend stopped, became quiet, turned and gently asked, "Dave, isn't this just about your pride? Isn't this just about your unwillingness to serve and humble yourself before someone who may have more experience and a better perspective?" That's when it happened.

As I write these words, they appear like normal sentences made up of customary vowels and consonants. But those words from my friend had an arresting effect. Suddenly, God had entered our silly argument and that faithful question pierced my heart as if spoken directly by the Holy Spirit. It was one of those rare moments — and, quite honestly, I haven't had many — where the clarity of a simple question felt like the convicting voice of God's assessment. Those words were a sledgehammer that crumpled my body and soul. A wave of conviction crest over me when I heard, "your pride." I knew he was right — thou art the man (2 Samuel

our roles for service, ensured each of us experienced genuine care, and made ministry a delight.

Plurality is God's means of leading the church to fulfill its purpose, but it's also a means of growing its leaders. The plurality became a slice of the church seeking to experience and apply, in a determined manner, what God was saying to the church. That's when the light bulb flipped on. *The quality of our plurality would determine the health of the church.* I knew that failing to lead with these men meant weaker souls and a weaker church. It meant potentially forfeiting the mission. But succeeding with them ensured a level of God glorifying success in our spiritual lives that would spill over into the lives of the congregation.

Plurality Counterfeits

We have some exciting terrain to cover ahead. We'll explore what it means to build and maintain a healthy plurality. But before we move forward we must address a hard reality. Plurality is one of those words where teams can use the vocabulary but really don't understand the language. This lack of clarity creates dangerous leadership cultures that praise the principle but misapply the practice. Out of this springs counterfeit pluralities — certain forgeries imitating the real thing.

Let's look at a few:

Counterfeit # 1 — Expert-Grabbing Pluralities

I'm grateful to God for the array of specialized gifts and ministries God has placed in the body of Christ. Let's face it:

Every local church needs some access to lawyers, counselors, consultants, seminary professors, and leadership or network coaches. These people, their ministries, and spiritual gifts can sharpen elders, supply essential perspectives, and help elders better understand how to wisely steward their role.

But these ministries exist to supplement, not replace, the plurality of local church elders. Thankfully, most of them know they do not hold a responsibility before God for the local church, the elders do. Practically, this means their expertise should never "expert" out the wisdom, prayer, and deliberation of God's appointed shepherds, "in which the Holy Spirit has made you overseers (elders), to care for the church of God" (Acts 20:28).

One area where "expert-grabbing" is particularly acute is when pastors and elders — particularly lead pastors— immediately reach for outside help to the exclusion of their local elders. This has been a significant issue in many of the 'Celebrity pastor' tumbles. They maintain the appearance of accountability and discipleship without ever having to do the hard-but-necessary work of being loved and challenged by people who know them best. But in defining moments of ministry, leaving fellow-pastors at arms-length while outsourcing pastoral care undermines one critical strength that pluralities can offer — care for one another. And the greatest casualty of this arrangement is authentic accountability. Accountability at a distance can never replace local friendship and plurality.

Guys, make no mistake. We can't preach local church care to our congregations and then exempt ourselves from the same care.

One of the quickest ways for a lead pastor to undermine a healthy plurality is to communicate to the leaders around him that, though they are a part of his team, they are insufficient for the care and health of his soul. If Jesus is comfortable being called our brother (Hebrews 2:11), then no one is too great to avoid being a brother to someone else. To use the words of 1 Peter 5: 1, we must live as "fellow elder(s)." Again, I'm not trying to exclude outside help; I use it myself. But the gift of outside help is meant to be received in partnership with the local elders. We always want to ensure the men to whom we are accountable know what is being advised, prescribed, corrected, or even celebrated. More on this below, so let's move to the second counterfeit.

Counterfeit # 2 — Reluctant Pluralities

A reluctant plurality happens when the men assembled do not understand their role or see the significance of their role before God. Each elder possesses an authority from God to serve as a shepherd, guide, and protector of their church by rightly applying the Word of God.[12] They may delegate authority to lead pastors, directional or executive elders, or empower committees

> **Reluctant pluralities rarely experience genuine accountability.**

when the occasion calls for it. But as a member of an eldership plurality, each elder possess an equal share of God-given authority for the church.[13]

---

[12] 2 Timothy 2:15; Titus 1:9–11.
[13] Acts 20:28; 1 Thessalonians 5:12–13; 1 Timothy 3:5; Hebrews 13:7.

Reluctant pluralities do not evaluate ministries, meetings, or labor for the good of their members. Or when they do, their words are often so mitigated that the points for constructive criticism get lost. Reluctant pluralities rarely experience genuine accountability. As a result, they are often dominated by the strongest personality, whose other title is typically "Lead Pastor." This is not about an elder speaking more, though an elder who rarely speaks should probably re-examine either his courage or his call.

Strong leaders need a cadre of courageous men willing to name the BS when something starts to smell funny. Reluctant pluralities create the illusion of accountability, with little true accountability. These groups often devolve into an entourage of friends and family so enamored with certain elders' gifts, fruit, or leadership instincts. This enamored entourage can easily become a group of enablers — people who have something stroked in them by cutting the leader some slack. Every leader must eventually realize that sometimes accommodating team members may be great encouragers, but they are often poor correctors. When this dynamic is present and unacknowledged, together the plurality becomes an increasingly reluctant plurality.

Counterfeit # 3 — Unnecessary Pluralities

There's an unexpected and complicated assumption that can undermine the experience of genuine plurality. This is often a notion beholden to talented lead pastors: *The more gifted the leader, the less necessary the plurality.*

Let's not oversimplify this forgery or reflexively assume men with greater gifts are just less humble. It's more nuanced and diagnostically complex. Interdependence and collaboration emerge from a sober realization of limitations and a sense that the ideas and wisdom needed for guiding a church is beyond a single man's capacity. Sharing ministry with others, therefore, seems desirable, natural, necessary, fruitful, and even a relief. The conviction about the wisdom of many being greater than one man's genius seems instinctively correct.

However, the leader of many talents has walked a different road. Somewhere in his journey he discovered that he grasps things more quickly than others, can diagnose problems more accurately, retain information more easily, express ideas more clearly, galvanize people more naturally, or win a room over with a more charming candor. His experience has trained him to assume that, when given the space to lead and freedom to control, he can typically accomplish his goals. If you're a multiplication whiz, time spent waiting for others to arrive at the correct answer seems like "down-time," even wasted time. You already have the answer.

Likewise, high capacity leaders may believe they already have the best answers and the team is just an obstacle to him. Similar to the star running back who believes he can gain yards if he just has the ball, the leader forgets how others are blocking in order for him to shine so bright. This delusion may last for

The man who needs no one will soon be alone.

a while, until either the star breaks down or the other teammates atrophy altogether from lack of use or care. The man who needs no one will soon be alone.

These sorts of leaders often emerge cultivating, and then operating within a dangerous inconsistency. Plurality is certainly a good idea; it's just less necessary for him.

This is why gifted leaders can sometimes have difficulty keeping good people around them. Collaboration and connection seems inefficient; other leaders seem less necessary and their gifts less impressive. When a strong leader has a revolving door of guys under his leadership, it typically means he doesn't play well in the plurality sandbox. On the other hand, when gifted leaders can keep leaders, it's typically because they comprehend their need for the other elders.

For a gifted man to have a strong plurality, he must be willing to walk a self-emptying path. This includes listening eagerly as differently-gifted people provide perspective, analyze situations, express care, or even attempt to correct him. For people with unique talents and unusual qualities, collaboration can feel like a restrictor plate on a NASCAR engine instead of a gift for greater mission effectiveness. Sometimes, in fact, it just might be that. But your speed is less important to God than how you race (1 Corinthians 9:24).

A highly-gifted leader who exercises wisdom will understand they're called to more than faster and bigger. When these leaders remain flexible and are eager to learn, they can adopt the wiser principle: *The more gifted the man, the more essential the plurality*. Gifted men can be more vulnerable to autonomy, control, self-worship, and arrogance.[14] But healthy collaborators hold up the mirror of godliness to each other and invite one another to peer intently at what they see.

---

[14] Proverbs 16:8; 27:2; 29:1; Luke 18:9–14; Romans 12:3; Philippians 2:3; James 1:19; 4:6.

Instead of falling for self-deception, plurality makes us see ourselves in the eyes of honest men. An eldership becomes healthier when they remind one another of their humanity, their fragility, their limitations, finitude, weaknesses, and ultimately their need for God. This escorts us back to how God defines success. Success is not rooted in our endowments, but revealed in how we humbly steward God's gifts among the community of his saints and before the watching world.

PRINCIPLES

CREATING A HEALTHY PLURALITY

Let's return again to the fundamental point driving this book, *the quality of your plurality will determine the health of your church.* With this fresh in our minds again, let's look at the components of a healthy plurality.

Pluralities are healthy when they satisfy certain fundamental obligations. To meet these fundamental obligations a plurality must embrace five essential principles:

- Model Roles and Mutual Submission
- Meet Regularly to Govern Well
- Provide a Context for Care
- Enjoy Accountability
- Pursue "Outside Partnership"

When a plurality embraces these five principles, it helps create health that spills over into the church. You may not agree or assign the same value to each of these, but here's how it looks in our little world at Sojourn Network.

Model Roles and Mutual Submission

A plurality is not an egalitarian enterprise that denies individual gifting, removes roles, or demands equality in function. For pluralities to be healthy, we need to recognize each man is made in the image of God. We all process reality differently, but together we create a group personality. We all possess diverse gifts making us suitable for unique roles. Made in the image of God, human beings are patterned after the Trinity, who operates with unity of the Godhead, diversity of persons, and a blessed harmony together. We live out unity in Christ and common confession. We enjoy diversity in giftings and perspective as we strive by the Spirit for maturity, aspiring to blessed harmony.[1] One member may have a stronger mission impulse pressing the team to consider the lost, both local and abroad. Another may have financial skills to advise the team on income projections, financial accountability, and how to budget wisely. The beauty of plurality is that God assembles remarkably unique individuals to become a unique gospel culture.

Perhaps the most strategic role to the health of the plurality is the person appointed to lead the plurality. Though the authority for the church inheres in the entire eldership, a wise eldership will look for one among them with the character, leadership and public ministry skills to fulfill the

---

[1] Adapted from the Collaboration chapter of Daniel Montgomery and Jared Kennedy's *Leadership Mosaic: 5 Leadership Principles for Ministry and Everyday Life*, (Wheaton: Crossway, 2016).

role of lead pastor. To this man they delegate[2] the necessary authority to cultivate the unity and growth of the plurality, to lead the plurality into wise decision-making, to help the elders assume proper responsibility and accountability within the varying aspects and ministries of the church (including for himself as fellow elder). The primary role of the lead pastor is the stewardship of these dynamics within the plurality before God and in service of the congregation.

Where Is a Lead Pastor in Scripture?

Now admittedly, there is no single "killer" verse decisively justifying the appointment for the lead pastor. Rather, the role is derived from a broad pattern of order resonant in God and Scripture. The Old Testament offers a gallery of names that remind us of God's practice of using *one* to influence *many* — Noah, Abraham, Moses, David, Nehemiah, Jeremiah — the list could fill many pages.

In New Testament times, we are informed that Christ chose the Twelve (Luke 6:12–16), but ordained Peter to fill a uniquely prominent role. The Jewish synagogues were ruled by a council of elders, yet each council had a chairperson or "ruler of the synagogue."[3] The early church enjoyed a plurality of leadership, yet it appears that James exerted a unique role and influence.[4] In the Trinity there is a head,[5] and in the home

---

[2] ". . . the permission for that person (the senior pastor) to lead comes from a plurality of leaders." Bill Hull, *The Disciple-Making Pastor: Leading Others on the Journey of Faith,* (Grand Rapids: Baker Books, 2007), 84.

[3] Luke 8:41; Acts 18:8, 17.

[4] Acts 15:13; 21:18; 1 Corinthians 15:7; Galatians 1:19; 2:12.

[5] John 1:1; 5:19; 12:49; 20:21; 1 Corinthians 11:3; 15:24–28; Ephesians 5:23.

there is a "head" (Ephesians 5:23). These examples, and many others, illustrate the notion that biblical leadership, though shared, is frequently organized and facilitated by a central figure.

But again, the lead pastor does not occupy this role because God sprinkled extra authority upon his life. He has a greater stewardship of the group's authority, responsibility,

A lead pastor's warrant to lead comes from the plurality.

and accountability. Furthermore, any temptation to believe his role is uniquely sacrificial compared to other elders can be quickly disabused by simply filling the shoes of another team member. Fathers who make assumptions about the "burdens of dad" often have their assumptions capsized after swapping the care-taking role with his wife for a day. Similarly, lead pastor's burdens are greeted with grace to carry their load.[6] But we can't underestimate the importance of the one appointed by the eldership to walk the fine lines of authority, responsibility, and accountability as he leads the elders towards collaborative leadership and decision making.

Someone must engage the reality that elders will at times be divided in their opinions, and the lead pastor must be given

---

[6] Effective senior pastors also lead aware that it is often more difficult to be submitted than to lead. Churchill's words should echo in the ears of every senior pastor, "In any sphere of action there can be no comparison between the positions of number one and numbers two, three, or four... The duties and problems of all persons other than number one are quite different and in many ways more difficult." Winston Churchill, *The Second World War, Volume II: Their Finest Hour*, (Boston: Houghton Mifflin Company, 1949), 14.

enough freedom and trust to advocate a plan to stir faith in the elders. By appointing him to the role of lead pastor, the elders are delegating an authority to serve the team for the good of church and never for the lead pastor alone.

But again, his warrant to lead comes from the plurality. There may even be times where the lead pastor may disagree with the elders' final decision, but will nevertheless be duty-bound to represent their position without hesitation.

For instance, when the leadership of Bethlehem Baptist convened to arrive at a position on divorce and remarriage, John Piper disagreed with the elders on certain features of their final position. Yet the doctrinal position adopted by Bethlehem Baptist Church was the one affirmed by the plurality of elders, not the one advocated by John Piper. Now stop and think about this: John Piper led the church through a process of affirming a position that he did not fully affirm himself. But because the plurality of elders affirmed and adopted it, Piper was conscience-bound to execute the will of the elders, though he was wisely afforded the opportunity by the elders to explain where he dissented.

The point? John Piper — the modern day prince of preachers — didn't assume his role as lead pastor granted him an extra portion of authority to overrule the elders. While we may be tempted to see a man with a respected name, a long tenure, incalculable book sales, and a growing social media following, he knew his role existed to represent the plurality, even when he disagreed.

Historically, the concept of a "leader leading leaders" has been captured by the Latin phrase *primus inter pares*,[7] "first among equals."[8] The phrase reflects that pluralities are an assembly of co-equal parties; yet each one decides to subordinate himself to a leader. Pluralities do this because they believe the "equals" are most effective when they have a "first" to tend the plurality and move them forward. Because of this self-emptying display of humility that the elders embrace (Philippians 2:5–11), the lead pastor becomes "first among equals."[9]

---

[7] "Primus inter pares — 'first among equals' — refers to a certain primacy, even among equals." James T. Bretzke, *Consecrated Phrases: A Latin Theological Dictionary: Latin Expressions Commonly Found in Theological Writings,* (Collegeville: The Liturgical Press, 1998), 96.

[8] "Therefore, those among the elders who are particularly gifted leaders and/or teachers will naturally stand out among the other elders as leaders and teachers within the leadership body. This is what the Romans called *primus inter pares*, meaning 'first among equals'." (Strauch, *Biblical Eldership*, 45).

[9] Reverend Eleazer Savage offers us a Baptist perspective on this term from the mid-nineteenth century saying, "The want of united action among the different presbyters of the same church when they were all of equal authority,' and the order of public deliberations requiring that there should be some one 'invested at least with the authority of collecting the sentiments and executing the resolutions' of the church, led to the appointment of one of their number a permanent president or moderator. The title bishop, which was applied to all the elders, came after a while to be applied exclusively to the president — elder, as Justin in the middle of the second century still calls him — merely to distinguish him from his equal co-elders. He was not superior to them, but only 'first among equals'." William Williams, *Apostolical Church Polity* (Philadelphia: American Baptist Publication Society, 1874) quoted in ed. Mark E. Dever ed., *Polity: A Collection of Historic Baptist Documents* (Washington, D.C.: Center for Church Reform, 2001), 532.

But there's a catch: This entire system occupies a tenuous place within a humility-protected tension. On one side is the lead pastor advocating for the opinions and involvement of the plurality, meaning he is pressing to obtain counsel and understand their thinking. On the other side is a plurality of elders creating space for the lead pastor to actually lead. This means they grant appropriate autonomy, choose to be an adaptable and congenial group, and recognize healthy plurality always embraces an ambiguous sense that we are limited creatures in every way. The result is a beautiful blending of teamwork where the elders remain jealous to protect the "primus" and the lead pastor knows he needs the "pares." In this exquisite, ambiguous, dynamic tension between "primus" and "pares" is where practical unity is founded on a bedrock of trust and humility with health flowing as a result.[10]

Meet Regularly to Govern Well

For a plurality to properly lead a local church, there must be meetings. This point typically elicits a collective groan. But regularly scheduled, agenda-guided, time-respected, attendance-required meetings are part of leading the local church with cohesion and

When leaders gather, God is present and always has his own agenda.

effectiveness. The agendas of these meetings should consistently reveal that the elders understand their call to

---

[10] If you want to read more on the role of the lead pastor, see the Sojourn Network white paper titled, "Why Lead Pastor?"

govern the church, not micromanage the details of church life. The discussion in these meetings should be vigorous, but always aware that resolutions and decisions are not always immediately available. A wise plurality recognizes the most effective use of their meetings will be from agendas discussing mission-critical matters to protect the doctrine and advance the mission of the church.

But we must remember when leaders gather, God is present and always has his own agenda. So we launch into our items in faith recognizing we must be adaptable and responsive when God reveals his own items for the gathering.

Plurality does not mean that every elder needs to be equally involved in every decision. Plurality does not trump wise, biblical themes like deploying gifts wisely, delegating responsibilities, time-management and decision-making. In a healthy plurality, equal authority does not mean equal responsibility for every area. Pluralities can and should consider ways of organizing themselves so trusted elders can have the right gifts matched to the right responsibilities with meetings attended by the right people. An effective lead pastor can be an enormous help in this endeavor.

Sometimes elders arrive at clarity by passing through the crucible of complexity.

When elders meet, opinions are their tools of the trade — the instruments through which they govern. This does not require each elder to express opinions on every decision. As an elder grows more comfortable in the group and more confident in their role, he eventually finds wise paths through the conflicted divide of saying too little versus saying too much. But he must live aware of strong temptations to find a political middle where he is simply withholding his opinions to protect how he is perceived. Such a practice denies the purpose of his role and weakens the unity and leadership of the local church. It's also helpful to remember that silence in the face of major decisions is typically counted as consent.

This means healthy pluralities should anticipate disagreements, even dissent. Rather than weakening the plurality, dissent displays the strength and health of a plurality. Dissent declares when unique individuals collaborate, the clash of ideas can create more ambiguity. Sometimes it pleases God for elders to arrive at clarity by passing through the crucible of complexity. When this happens, dissent may surface within the process. And while that may sound like a device of the enemy to divide the church, the presence of dissent can bear beautiful fruit in the elders and church.

To return to the illustration above, it's unlikely the members in Bethlehem Baptist Church thought the eldership was undermined by John Piper's dissent. On the contrary, seeing strong leaders who are willing to disagree, even while they humbly acknowledge that they may be wrong, actually deepens the confidence of a church in the integrity of the eldership. They know the unity of the elders is tested and informed, not simply a gesture of accommodation to the more vocal members or the mindless results of a predictable groupthink.

Can dissent be a sign of pride? You bet. It certainly was for me in the illustration where I opposed the appointment of the lead pastor. But the value of knowing where everybody stands is greater than the fear of falling into pride. Healthy elderships understand dissent must be explored; even if it reveals the group is valuing ease over engagement. Or perhaps it reveals the sinful heart of the dissenter. Just like it did with me.

Let's clarify one important point. Dissent is an "internal" privilege exercised in the context of plurality and their meetings. Dissent is not an "external" or public piece of information an elder relays to others to exempt himself from standing united with the elders or sharing the burden of the decision. One of the realities of a plurality is they sometimes make unpopular decisions. In those moments, the elders must stand united. Plurality can't thrive when it lives like a bad marriage when a big family decision goes poorly and one spouse points the finger at the other saying, "This was your idea." Few things can divide a church quicker than elders subtly telegraphing their disagreement with the unpopular decision of the other elders. The authority of eldership can tear down a church even quicker than it can build it up.

The elders must agree they serve God and the church first, therefore dissenters' names and opinions stay among the elders. When the elders speak, therefore, they do so with only one voice.

Provide a Context of Care

Our network bleeds soul care. Soul care is the belief that ministry flows from the inside out. Beneath it lays the gospel-inspired idea that our ministry is only as fresh as our connection to Jesus Christ. Lasting in ministry means we must know our heart and know how God's Word speaks to what we see. God loves us so much that he unites us into teams to experience community and love towards each other. This means we provide care for each other and receive care from each other.

The best care is local care received from a community who knows you and tracks your joys and temptations. The pastor who travels may look good from his preaching and pastoral presence, but the men around him at home are a better indicator of the true measure of the man. Recently I heard an interview with a fallen celebrity pastor expressing regret over not having older leaders on his care team comprised of people exclusively outside of his church. I couldn't help thinking there may be an additional lesson yet to be learned: True care starts with those who know us best; those to whom God has united us through the plurality. Outside help does not replace the plurality but works "in conjunction" with local church care.

In fact, local care is so important to God there is one elder set apart from the group to own responsibility for it — the lead pastor. Honestly, this remains pretty simple. If you want the local church to be a place of care, make sure the lead pastor is authorized to ensure the elders are receiving soul care. No one is in a better position to own this responsibility. The lead pastor can

> **Lead pastors, if your elders are not experiencing care, it's on you.**

prioritize it from the pulpit, make sure it makes meeting agendas, illustrate it from his sermons, and help build the church calendar with soul care in mind.

This mandate has implications for the entire plurality. Lead pastors, if your elders are not experiencing care, that's your failure. It's happening on your watch. From an organizational standpoint, you are responsible for their care. But before any elders are feeling too neglected, let me express the opposite side of this same principle: Elders, if your lead pastor is not receiving care, or is constantly having to find it outside of the eldership without you knowing or inquiring, that's your failure. It's happening on your watch.

Maybe you're reading this as a lead pastor of a large church and you are now freaking out because it's physically impossible to assume care for thirty elders. My point is not that you have to actually do it yourself or by yourself. My point is that you are responsible to ensure it's being done. This means you must not only ensure that the systems and structures are created, but that they are also working fruitfully.

One last thing: I'm intentionally accenting the idea of not only "receiving" care but also "providing" care. I make this distinction because I've noticed a trend, particularity among younger leaders, where soul care is reduced to "a need met in me" rather than "a ministry that flows from me." In other words, soul care is perceived selfishly — it's first something I need rather than being first something I offer to others.

In my travels, I'm constantly running into leaders who are starving for soul care. They feel a gaping hole in their life because of the absence of initiative towards them or care for them. To them I say, soul care is not first something you receive, it's something that you give. Soul care is not a culture you assume, it's a culture you build. And it starts with them reaching out, opening their homes, taking an interest, and loving those they lead. Then, over time, as we invest in creating a culture of care rather than assuming a culture of care, a remarkable thing happens. We become the objects of care to others even as we've been caring for them. Jesus said it best, "And as you wish that others would do to you, do so to them" (Luke 6:31).

Enjoy Accountability

Guys, let's face it. If a pastor's accountability isn't in the local church, it's probably not real accountability. It's the illusion of accountability so we can traffic in the vocabulary without the entanglements of the substance.

> **If a pastor's accountability isn't in the local church, it's probably not real accountability.**

Here's the problem: Not everyone is clear on what they mean when they use the word "accountability." Let me suggest four specific values we should seek to experience in accountability of plurality.

1. Intentionality
2. Self-Disclosure
3. Approachability
4. Appeal

Below we'll look a bit at each of these values. But before we do, there is one overarching principle we must never overlook. If you want to know the secret underlying the kind of loving, accountable relationships where elders grow more in love with Jesus, their wife, and their ministry, it's humility. That's right, humility.

An Important Word on Humility

Humility is the oil that lubricates the engine of plurality. When one considers all of the polity options God could have chosen for governing churches, I theorize that God chose plurality because he loves humility.[11] And plurality can't work without humility because, in plurality, God imposes a governing structure that can't be effective without embodying humble values. God loves unity, so he calls us to plurality where we must humbly persevere with one another to function effectively. God loves making us holy, so he unites us to men who will make us grow. God loves patience, so he imposes a way of governing that requires humble listening and a trust that he is working in the lives of others.

God has decided the church will be governed in ways that value both the ends and the means. That is, God values decision making, but he also values the way we relate to each other in the decision-making process. We often think what's "best" in polity is what's most efficient, easiest, or most effective way of doing something. Instead, God's best way is whatever is the most beautiful way. The standard of beauty is God, specifically the interplay of his own unity, diversity, and harmony. God throws together diverse men with different gifts who have strong opinions and then insists upon their unity. This does not always look or feel "beautiful." But God

---

[11] 2 Chronicles 34:27; Proverbs 11:2; 22:4; 29:23; Micah 6:8; Matthew 18:1–4; 23:10–12; Ephesians 4:1–3; Philippians 2:3–4; James 4:6, 10; 1 Peter 5:5–6.

still charges elders to lead the church. As they lead, they are also called to grow in their exercise of authority as they remain mutually accountable and responsible to one another. The only hope for such a dynamic to exist in a group is for us to make humility our aim.

> But this is the one to whom I will look:
>> he who is humble and contrite in spirit
>> and trembles at my word. (Isaiah 66:2)

God made healthy plurality dependent upon accountability because he loves humility. Now we'll turn our attention to the four values of accountability, the first one being "intentionality."

Intentionality means I will have some defined, regular, and consistent context in my life where guys who know me can encourage me, pray for me, and understand my patterns of temptation. It's saying, "I love my wife enough, my family enough, the church enough, and fear God enough, that I'm actually going to define the contexts for my accountability. And rather than sharing in a generic manner, or in vague generalities, or using amoral words to remove any sense of my own moral agency, I'm going to ensure they know me all the way down to where I am most tempted. This way they can pray for me, encourage my growth, and ask about how I'm doing." We must press down into all the areas that could potentially detonate our family or ministry and define when and where these will be discussed. That's intentionality.

Self-Disclosure means while you are always welcome to inquire about my soul, it is not your job to investigate my life, my sin, or my temptations. Self-disclosure brings forth humility by making it our responsibility to humbly open our souls to those to whom we are accountable. Fellow elders are not prosecuting attorneys cross-examining your life. Instead, you are a witness to your own life, sharing truthfully, freely, and happily with little or no provocation. In Christ, we have God's self-disclosure (John 1:18). Jesus is God moving towards us making himself known. Self-disclosure stems from the incarnation by communicating we too want to experience deep community. We move towards one another by beginning with making ourselves known first. The burden is on me to disclose my joys and struggles.

This small distinction in how we view self-disclosure results in a far more gracious approach to accountability and respects the believer's relationship with God. Behind this value is a confidence that God's work in our lives propels us towards an honest life before him and one another. Placing the accent on our disclosure creates an arrangement where accountability is not rigged to find sin or places us in the role of the Holy Spirit. Rather, it is transformed into a context to trust God's Word and encourage the exercise of humility. When I make self-disclosure my responsibility it's easier for others to ask me questions about my soul, my marriage, my parenting, my ministry, or to share their heart for me.

Approachability is best described by Ken Sande who writes about the importance of conducting ourselves in a way that makes us approachable, generous, and easy to talk to — even if our conversation is about something hard. Sande says when we live humbly, resonate with openness, and become more Christ-like, we gain "passports" into the lives of others.

This is an important concept for anyone who wants to experience genuine, meaningful, and fruitful accountability.

Simply belonging to a group is not a passport into the lives of others. A passport, remember, is an authorization to enter and travel in a foreign land. Similarly as we are intentional, self-disclosing and approachable with one another, we gain passports into the lives of the other people in our group. These "passports" are earned bestowals of trust that come when others feel they can trust us with their own self-disclosure and with the care of their souls amidst their struggles.

If you want to experience real accountability and helpful feedback from others, you will need to be known as one who is approachable and trustworthy.

Appeal recognizes accountability is hard and sometimes needs help. Maybe the experience of fellowship breaks down due to a conflict that can't be resolved, or maybe one person in the group feels permanently tagged by something they've confessed. Maybe it's something more serious: You seem to be caught in sin and the group feels unable to help, or your wife feels trapped by some pattern of behavior you're exercising in the home and just doesn't know what to do. The value of appeal says, even before we start our group, we

> **If you want to experience real accountability, be approachable and trustworthy.**

are agreeing a plea for help may be necessary and we are defining the person or group within the church to whom we will appeal. Appeal says that seeking outside help is not betrayal or slander, but sometimes necessary when sinners are trying to help each other. Appeal says we are agreeing up front we will not allow our homes to become tightly controlled, closed systems; that our wives can appeal to others for help if they feel it is needed. Our cycles of accountability can be appealed if something becomes an albatross. The value of appeal anticipates that sometimes we are blind and need help and in that moment, we are far less likely to want to seek it. So we agree now to protect ourselves (and those we love) then.

Pursue "Outside Partnership"

This is where I risk sounding a little schizophrenic. I'm not attempting to confuse you with inconsistent ideas. Scripture and experience tell us that local church elderships sometimes need outside help. A strong belief in plurality doesn't ensure a given team is entirely self-sufficient or possesses all they need for every situation. Pluralities are healthy to the degree that they recognize their interdependence upon others outside of their church can help them maximize their strengths and bring aid to their weaknesses. Like churches, a plurality should never be an independent entity (1 Corinthians 12:12–18).

Though the church in Philippi clearly defined plurality of elders and deacons (Philippians 1:1), it was also vitally connected with another ministry outside their local church. They were connected to Paul and his team. Paul refers to this connection as their "partnership in the gospel from the first day until now" (1:5). There's a principle to remember here — the Philippians were a strong, established church with established elders and deacons. But the strength and health of their leadership did not move them towards independence from outside help. They recognized that the goal of church maturity didn't involve a disconnected and self-sufficient eldership. On the contrary, the Philippians shared Paul's burdens and vice-versa.[12] The bottom line is: maturity for the Philippians resulted in stronger interdependence and a cooperative relationship with others.

Paul counted on many helpers in his ministry, many of whom were elders themselves.[13] And throughout Paul's ministry travels, we see this beautiful pattern repeated: Paul establishes a church in a new location, he moves on to plant another church in a new city or region. But Paul doesn't just "move on" to the next ministry opportunity. He returns to previously planted churches to further cultivate his connection with their plurality of elders. When church leaders had specific questions (1 Corinthians 7:1–7), Paul was seen as an "Outside Source" to appeal to for help and guidance. The same pattern continued with Paul's many helpers.

Every plurality should strive to enjoy the kind of fruitful interdependence that reproduces this biblical pattern. "The narrative of Paul's missionary work," writes Eckhard

---

[12] See Philippians 2:9–30; 4:10–20.

[13] Barnabas, Titus, and Timothy all assist Paul, seem to be elders themselves, and are charged to identify and raise up elders (see Acts 14:23; 15:2–4, and Paul's letters of 1 Timothy and Titus). Thus only qualified and approved elders should fulfill the role of raising up additional elders. Therefore, one qualification of an elder must be at least the probable ability to understand elder qualifications, evaluate others in light of them, and instruct other men in these elder qualifications.

Schnabel, "provides a paradigm, a model for the mission of the church."[14] Paul's ministry shows us a pattern for the interdependence between local leaders and outside help available through denominations and networks.

But let's face it. When sinners gather, problems abound. When problems erupt within the church, elderships are the first line of service and care. But sometimes elderships become fragmented over how to interpret or handle a local church issue. Experience and history also remind us there are times where weaknesses, biases, or cultural limitations in the plurality can hinder their ability to deal with certain kinds of complexities. There is rarely a problem in a local church that is unique — it's just particular to this church at this moment. But we can get stuck in tunnel vision when problems arise. This is all the more reason for pluralities to be devoted to ongoing growth in doctrine and wisdom with trustworthy outside influences. If a plurality remains too rigid in these areas, they can become entrenched in unhealthy thinking or lead with poor solutions and the local church will suffer.

I'm a local church guy and a card-carrying plurality participant for over three decades. But there are times, quite honestly, where the plurality is part of the problem, not the solution. In times like this, it's vital for the elders to seek and obtain outside help from those who know their world. A mature eldership anticipates these moments and creates procedures for identifying those sources of help. As an example, within the Sojourn Network, we are a second line of help for counsel, perspective, or advice when pluralities are at

---

[14] Eckhard Schnabel, *Paul the Missionary: Realities, Strategies and Methods,* (Downers Grove: IVP Academic, 2008), 377.

an impasse. We don't lord over a local church, rather we aim to serve as a loving partner to the local church. Just over the past few months, we've assessed church planters, and helped lead pastors transition in and out of roles. We've also offered a range of advice on mission strategies and assisted churches in understanding how to better position men within their plurality. We've consulted on how to wisely merge two different congregations, and offered some counseling expertise for some nuanced and complicated local church situations. We've finalized a book series to develop equipping tools for pastors, and advised teams on how to be more effective in roles ranging from children's ministry leaders, to executive pastors, to elders and deacons who help build care structures within a local church.

More important than any of those particular tasks though is the essential feature of our mission as a network: to help local church leaders build and maintain healthy pluralities. Quality pluralities embedded and leading within the Sojourn Network is a primary way we can know we are fulfilling our mission.

If the quality of your plurality determines the health of your church, then every church needs to partner with a trustworthy group outside of their local church who can help them cultivate and protect the quality of that plurality.

PROCESS

MAINTAINING A HEALTHY PLURALITY

Once a plurality of leadership is in place, it requires a philosophy of ministry that involves inspection and maintenance to remain healthy. Pluralities exist in a paradox: they are both delicate and durable. On the one hand, it's a group of men called to be a source of such strength and weight bearing to lead a church forward against all odds, governments, cultures, sin, and the Devil himself. At the same time, they bear an impossible commission to reach the world and push back the darkness of sin. Yet in a very real way, a plurality can easily fall apart. There is always the danger of running aground in an argument. They can lose sight of the most important things and end up focusing on peripheral issues. A plurality is not a "set-it-and-forget-it" recipe. Rather, it's delicate, powerful machinery that needs regular inspection and care.

We've already given an overview of the counterfeits of pluralities and what it takes to build healthy pluralities. Now let's explore what will help a plurality on the long haul. We'll use the inspection of a four-cylinder engine as a metaphor. A cylinder is a giant tube in the engine where the piston moves up and down to compress the gas and ignite the combustion. (If that doesn't sound right, blame Google — I only know on which side of the car the gas cap is located). My point is that there are four plurality cylinders that power the engine of the team. When these cylinders are working well together, the team engine starts easily and accelerates quickly to help the church move forward.

In the state where I grew up, cars had to be inspected once a year. Inspections were always a hassle, but through the inspection the owner learned what component of the car needed attention or replacement. This was a good process for new drivers because they learned that inspections help maintain the car, keep you safe, and keep the car moving forward.

Likewise, we should build (and join) an eldership with the same expectation. Starting with these four cylinders (agreement, trust, care, fit) should help. We need to inspect these four cylinders regularly. Remember, finding a problem is not an indictment on the leadership or the quality of the church. Where there are pluralities, there are inevitably problems (just like any car will need maintenance). The wise team is the one who minimizes these problems through regular inspection.

If our discussion of principles is how to build a plurality, take the coming discussion of some of the same values as an inspection of how to discern the health of your plurality.

Let's examine each plurality cylinder below and consider a few warning signs that may come across the dashboard.

Inspecting the Plurality: The Four-Cylinder Engine

How do we know if a plurality is healthy? A shallow definition of plurality can be nothing more than the names appearing in incorporating documents or under the "elders" tab on the church website. But healthy plurality embodies values, mutual respect, history of relationships, network affiliation, and constitutional responsibility. Embodying these values takes effort and time; a plurality cannot magically create a band of brothers. All leadership teams create particular cultures. Wherever two or more elders are gathered, culture emerges. The only question

> **As the elders go, so goes the church.**

is whether that culture fosters a healthy team — based on the above-mentioned values — resulting in a stronger church.

The importance of keeping plurality cannot be overstated. Like it or not, the culture of an eldership determines the health of a church. John MacArthur says, "Whatever the leaders are, the people become." This is not to diminish the role of the Holy Spirit, biblical preaching, the priority of mission, or many other means of grace that shape the people of God. But without the agency of healthy pluralities, each of these can be quenched or curtailed. As the elders go, so goes the church.

The Agreement Cylinder

Indicator: Do we agree with each other?

Many well intentioned — and faithful! — men have sought to build a church around over-simplified belief statements such as, "We believe in Jesus. Period." This serves neither the church, who looks to leaders for clarity, nor the elders who live in confusion over what truly unites them. A plurality grounded upon abstractions will never become a healthy team. When elders are united around the lowest common denominator, they find the agreement cylinder often breaks down at major decision-making points and this causes the engine to seize up.

A call to eldership includes defining and protecting the doctrinal borders of the church. Elders need not agree on everything, but they do need to be united on essential doctrines, beginning with the gospel. The church is a theological entity and therefore theological men united by theological agreement must lead it. This begins with a doctrinal unity grounded upon a statement of faith or some common creed(s) to which all subscribe (Ephesians 4:1–16). Some questions to evaluate the scope of your unity, and therefore inspect the Agreement Cylinder, include:

- Do we agree on what is meant by the word "gospel"? (1 Corinthians 2:2–5; 15:1–9; Galatians 1:6–12)
- Is the doctrinal basis of our unity as a team well defined?
- Do we have a statement of faith, and if so, do we all affirm our statement of faith? (Ephesians 4:1–16)
- Do our terms mean the same thing? (2 Timothy 2:13–14)

There's a second part to the Agreement Cylinder though; far more subtle yet no less important. It becomes apparent when you inspect how well the eldership talks about what they believe. Elderships become teams through timely, consistent, respectful, and vigorous theological discussion. Does your elder team employ care and wisdom when you discuss, debate, and differ on beliefs? Are you able to divide doctrines without dividing relationships? Some questions to monitor the quality of these conversations include:

- Are we growing together theologically through study and discussion? (2 Timothy 2:15)
- When we disagree on less important doctrines or methodologies, do we do it wisely and with love? (Ephesians 4:1–3)
- Is it clear to everyone that the elder team works hard to understand one another's positions and can represent them without exaggeration or misrepresentation? (James 1:19)

Some assume disagreement or dissent clog up the Agreement Cylinder. But it's a common fallacy that confuses dissent with disrespect or disloyalty. Humble elders who debate in ways that uphold the law of love actually improve the overall engine and performance of the team.[1] They know mindless uniformity among elders weakens the church.

---

[1] Jeffrey A. Sonnenfeld argues that a culture of open dissent is necessary for any leadership team to reach its potential and avoid the grave, common, and pesky dangerous decision-making of group think. Jeffrey A. Sonnenfeld, "What Makes Great Boards Great," *Harvard Business Review*, September, 2002.

They're able to comprehend a misguided deference to the loudest voice or the naïve admiration of a lead pastor and can see the dashboard warning lights.

In his bestselling book *Outliers*, Malcolm Gladwell tells the story of a commercial aircraft accident where the co-pilot was politely and deferentially suggesting course changes to the captain to avoid a collision. The more experienced captain readily dismissed the co-pilot's understated advice, quite possibly because the co-pilot was being too careful. The pilot never got the point. Minutes later, the aircraft splattered onto the side of a mountain. The point? Hyper-deference comes at a steep cost.

The Trust Cylinder

Indicator: Do we trust one another?

Trust lies at the heart of a healthy plurality. Each man must be convinced of the sincerity and integrity of the other. If doubt grows like mold in a basement, then soon the house will be toxic. Knowing the elders will speak honestly to the church, to each other, and to the lead pastor encourages them all to be vocal about their concerns and vulnerable about their weaknesses

Trust lies at the heart of a healthy plurality.

or temptations. Integrity deepens trust. Proverbs 10:9 says, "Whoever walks in integrity walks securely." Elders with integrity foster a culture of security.

One way to check the operation of the trust cylinder is to specifically measure confidence in loyalty. Some questions to spark the ignition for conversation include:

- Will you be loyal to God's Word by being completely honest with me? (Colossians 1:28–29)
- Will you judge me or exploit me when I show weakness? (Luke 6:37)
- Will you be patient with me in areas I need to grow? (1 Thessalonians 5:14)
- Can you be discreet once you really know my temptations? (Proverbs 3:21)
- Can I be confident you will not share what I confide in you with anyone who should not know?
- Do you have my back, but never for sin? (Proverbs 16:28)

To achieve genuine loyalty, each elder must be confident in how each team member will respond to the particulars of their fallenness. Remember, serving as an elder situates each man on a perch with a pretty good view into the lives of the other elders. You pray together, work together, think together, counsel together, rejoice together, assess together, and confess sins together. Sharing these experiences creates a clear view into the gifts, struggles, strengths, and weaknesses of the team. With this clear visibility, you stand armed with perspectives that can unite or divide, refine or weaken, build up or tear down. How you handle this visibility will determine whether men trust you.

Recently I sat with a small group of men confessing struggles of the past and fears of the future. When I'm confident of their loyalty, I'm better able to hear their wise corrections and compassion. Having this trust in turn liberates me to speak freely. Let's face it: Absent that kind of confidence, elders stay superficial lest their temptation or weaknesses become poker chips played against them in the future. But team means loyalty, and loyalty says, "I will encourage your strengths without ignoring or exploiting your weaknesses."

This leads to a second check for the trust cylinder: the presence of humility. To move from a plurality to a team, each man must realize they need the other men. They must experience and model Paul's analogy of the body (1 Corinthians 12:12–27), which assumes, "To grow, I need your help." Inspecting the presence of humility can start with a few simple questions:

- Are you quick to listen or quick to speak? (James 1:19)
- Will you withdraw when there is misunderstanding? (Matthew 5:23–24)
- Will you be humble if I risk correcting you? (Proverbs 9:8)

If community tests humility, then creating a team is like sitting for the bar exam — longer, trickier, and absent immediate results. But this humility is earned over time and comes through men who suspect themselves first and not others. With the passing of time, this becomes a rich oil that lubricates the relationships and powers the Trust Cylinder to help push the engine of team forward.

This Trust Cylinder — loyalty and humility — will help you navigate many treacherous seas. If you find yourself on turbulent waters right now, remember that the beauty and simplicity of the cylinder design is embedded in time-tested glory of the Golden Rule (Luke 6:31). As elders, we are simply agreeing to respond to life together in the same way we teach others to respond. And amazingly, as we apply this teaching, trust and loyalty abound.

For a plurality to become a team, agreement and trust are essential. Yet the truth is, your elder team and church can't survive on just these two cylinders. They'll carry you down the road for a few miles, but you'll eventually sputter out. Two more cylinders complete the engine and need inspection for the long haul: Care and Fit.

The Care Cylinder

Indicator: Do we care for each other?

Now we can see how each cylinder is connected to the others. How can a man be cared for by those he neither trusts nor seems to agree? The notion is unrealistic, and probably a little naïve. According to Jesus, it's our love for one another, not our productivity and performance, that is supposed to mark our distinction (John 13:34–35). When elders love one another, the channels of care open wide and shepherds enjoy the blessings of being shepherded.

God loves elders and he wants their souls to be nurtured and tended to. So he supplies sufficient grace to convert pluralities into teams. When a team identity begins to form, the care of each member becomes even more important.

What follows is review of material we covered in the previous section, "plurality counterfeits" from the first chapter, but it bears repeating again. In a world where almost anything can be professionalized and outsourced, it's easy for pastors to farm out their care by finding the primary help for their soul outside of the eldership, sometimes even outside of the church. We must build our primary network of care from within and then enjoy the delight that comes from a "neighbor who is near" (Proverbs 27:10b).

A wise elder understands this principle. We can't preach the principle that people should receive care through their local church pastors, then exempt ourselves from the same kind of care. As I said earlier, as elders go, so goes the church. When applied to care, this means the manner in which pastors receive care is the very method and model they reinforce for the church. The culture comes as each elder commits himself to providing care for others.

> **Care is not first something that elders get; it's something they give.**

Care is not first something that elders get; it's something they give. Care is not typically a culture you inherit; it's one you must build. A lead pastor can't assume a culture of care nor simply wish hopefully for it to appear — it must be constructed.

Elders, here are some questions that may help you assess how well your care cylinder is functioning:

- Is it clear to each of us that our state of soul matters to each other as much as (or more than!) our performance? (John 13:34–35)
- Are our conversations more likely to be filled with encouragement or critique? (Ephesians 4:29)

- Can we point out specific times (not merely once) where we talk about our lives, families, struggles and/or temptations (something apart from ministry!)? (James 5:16)

- Does my feedback on your performance include encouragement? (1 Thessalonians 5:11)

- Does someone on this team know the temptations to which I am vulnerable? (Galatians 6:2)

- Would my wife feel free to call you if I was tanking? Why or why not?

The Fit Cylinder

Indicator: Do we enjoy being with each other and know where we fit?

A team that enjoys one another unites around theological convictions, models genuine love towards each other, and enjoys the fruit of trust, agreement, and care working together in harmony. But there's one more thing. In fact this final cylinder is often overlooked, yet possesses the potential to shut down the other three when they are not operating together.

Elders need to know they fit. Not just "fitting in" but know they are a "fit" in their heart and mind. Tensions arise when a man desires a role to which he is not suited. A pastoral candidate whose personality does not mesh well with the team may dramatically shift the culture of the plurality and, indirectly, the entire church. "Fit" is perhaps the most complicated cylinder to assess, but perhaps these categories and questions will supply a way to measure it.

Endowment

Endowment is the idea that we are hardwired as created beings with certain strengths, talents, and proclivities. By following the path of endowment, we discover the kinds of roles, service, and people with whom we best fit. This path leads us into vineyards where we will find the largest fruit from our labors.

Some questions to evaluate endowment are:

- Though each elder is distinct, does my personality appear to mesh with these men?
- Are we able to work together in ways that deepen our relationships rather than strain them?
- Does our time together (or with a potential elder) incite greater joy and creativity in my role or frustration and discouragement?
- How well do we understand the gifts God has given each of us and how well are our responsibilities aligned with those gifts? (Romans 12:6)

Expectations

Healthy pluralities spring from defined roles and clarity on the hopes and expectations of the role. Questions to ask could include:

- Do I know my role and what is expected of me? (Acts 6:1–7)
- Do I have a written job description?
- Do I know to whom I report?

- How should I communicate to my co-laborers and elder in charge of this area?
- Is my commitment to serve the church thorough enough to support a change of roles? (Mark 10:45)

This cylinder's operation requires we dispense of any faux-spirituality, which resists strictly defining our ideas for a role or ministry. We must always define faith in a way that encourages us to be open, clear, and bold with our expectations. As servants of Christ committed to the best for his church, we realize sometimes our expectations or roles need to change to best serve the church. Maturity matters. This important principle is as old as the New Testament church.

In Acts 6, each widow had the daily attention of the apostles. It was a beautiful, organic, relational picture of a wonderful phase of the Jerusalem church. But growth happened and the organism had to organize. This meant the apostle's roles needed to change. The delivery of care to the widows would now come through different hands as the apostles needed to give their attention to more strategic service, namely, "prayer and the ministry of the word" (Acts 6:4).

Each day the apostles served in a particular, perhaps predictable way. They were among the people serving those with desperate needs. The expectations were clear. But as the church began to grow, their roles and expectations had to change. Sometimes it is for the better when we move on to duties we enjoy more. Other times it is service, where we empty ourselves and take the lower seat (Philippians 2:5–11;

Luke 14:10). For the Jerusalem church, the result was even greater fruit as "the word of God continued to increase, and the number of the disciples multiplied greatly in Jerusalem, and a great many of the priests became obedient to the faith" (Acts 6:7).

The point? When the Jerusalem church leaders found their fit and defined the expectations, it led to a healthier church and a people more satisfied in their service. Organizational discipline and adaptation becomes important for any church moving on toward health.

Evaluation

Last comes evaluation. To arrive at different roles, the leaders of the Jerusalem church had to engage in some touchy, seemingly dispassionate examination. Should the roles of those serving the widows be changed? This question was dangerous — widows were among the most vulnerable people in the land. God himself joins the discussion when the care of widows is evaluated (Psalm 68:5; Jeremiah 49:11; James 1:27). Nevertheless, these leaders engaged in a difficult assessment of their roles, their daily to-do lists, their responsibilities, and their gifts. From this Spirit-led evaluation came fruit and growth.

When one reads the requirements for elders or deacons, it's clear that "evaluation" is a doorway to ministry. When Paul tells Timothy to "keep a close watch on yourself and on the teaching" (1 Timothy 4:16), it's clear that evaluation doesn't end at the front door.

Here are some questions to help elderships inspect the place evaluation presently plays within their culture:

- Have we clearly defined how we will evaluate one another and what determines success?

- Am I aware of the specific and regular contexts where we will evaluate our fruitfulness as a team?

- Have we clarified the process by which I can share concerns about how I am being handled or assessed? (Titus 1:3–9)

Inspections and Progress

Central to all of this is the gospel with its God-preeminent, church-sacrificing, and flesh-killing claims. A healthy elder team won't happen overnight. You won't walk into the perfect situation, and you won't luck into it. Furthermore, it'll take hard work and dedication to keep it running once you enjoy health. You'll have to crucify your pride, push down your fears, and hold on to the promises. But in the end the fruit is sweet. The gospel works gloriously in your team and into the hearts of your congregation.

> A healthy elder team won't happen overnight. You'll have to crucify your pride, push down your fears, and hold on to the promises.

CONCLUSION

The goal of a plurality is not just starting strong. We want our churches to be missional and see God move in powerful ways. But heck, we want to finish the race. That's part of the reason why we've bound together in this brotherhood. We want to finish the race. The goal is not just starting strong; it's not growing fast. It's remaining together. This is why Paul's words in the Philippians 1:4–6 are so captivating:

> [In every prayer for all of you, I always pray] with joy, because of your partnership in the gospel from the first day until now. And I am sure of this, that he who began a good work in you will bring it to completion at the day of Jesus Christ.

What a great vision of what this should look like. This is a long-haul vision. It's worth keeping the four cylinders running smoothly and powering the engine of a maturing plurality. Why? Because the quality of your plurality determines the health of the church.

In closing, I have sought to uphold the principle of repetition passed along from my preaching professor. The primary point has been stated, repeated, and then reiterated. My task as a writer is complete. While your role as a more faithful plurality member may be just beginning. May God grant you grace to serve the church he loves that you might become the elder she needs!

PRACTICES

APPENDICES

APPENDIX ONE

BIBLICAL EVIDENCE FOR THE OFFICE OF ELDER AND ELDER PLURALITY AS NORMATIVE IN THE NEW TESTAMENT CHURCH

The New Testament uses the word for "elder" (πρεσβύτερος, and its variants), the word for "bishop/ overseer" (ἐπίσκοπος), and the noun form of "pastor" (ποιμήν, literally shepherd in the sense of sheep) or the verb instruction "to shepherd/pastor" (ποιμαίνω) interchangeably. This principle flows throughout the New Testament letters without contradiction, but can be quickly and succinctly observed in the following three passages:

- **Acts 20:** In Acts 20:17 Paul calls the elders (πρεσβύτερος) of Ephesus to himself and then addresses them as "bishop/overseer" (ἐπίσκοπος) in Acts 20:28, while in the same verse using pastor/shepherd language instructing them "to shepherd" (ποιμαίνω) with clear cognates of ποιμήν.

- **Titus 1:** Paul calls Titus to appoint elders (πρεσβύτερος) throughout Crete in Titus 1:5 and proceeds to describe the character and gifting of an elder. However, mid-way through Paul's list in verses 6–9, he switches the noun to "bishop/overseer" (ἐπίσκοπος) proclaiming, "For an *overseer,* as God's steward, must be above reproach." Paul finishes the list in Titus 1:9, but continues through Titus 1:9–16 by giving a similar pastoral admonition to Acts 20:28–30 about defending sound doctrine in the church as a means of protecting God's people.

- **1 Peter 5:** Peter exhorts his fellow elders (πρεσβύτερος) in 1 Peter 5:1–2 "to shepherd/pastor" (ποιμαίνω) the flock by exercising gentle "oversight," (ἐπισκοπέω) an obvious cognate to "bishop/overseer" (ἐπίσκοπος).

Therefore, while not an exhaustive list, these highlight the succinct passages where all three terms are used interchangeably by the same author in short succession which effectively ends any argument these terms are not synonymous.

While each of terms for elder ("elder" πρεσβύτερος, and its variants), "bishop/overseer" (ἐπίσκοπος), and "pastor" (ποιμήν) can appear in singular form, they never appear in New Testament letters in sense of governing, ruling or leadership of the church as a singular elder. Therefore, here is the exhaustive summary of the three terms in plurality (omitting non-local church Book of Revelation references):

Examples and Instruction of Elders in Plurality

Acts 14:23 — Elders are appointed to every church

Acts 15:6 — Elders and apostles resolve a major church doctrine issue of the gospel for Gentiles

Acts 20:28 — Overseers shepherd the flock in Ephesus

Ephesians 4:11 — Pastor/Shepherd is spoken as gift

Philippians 1:1 — Overseers written to by Paul

1 Timothy 4:14 — Council of elders laid hands on Timothy

1 Timothy 5:17 — Elders plurality to rule, preach, and teach

Titus 1:5 — Titus is instructed by Paul to appoint a plurality of elders

James 5:14 — Elders are to pray for the sick

1 Peter 5:1 — Peter instructs elders as a fellow elder

1 Peter 5:2 — Peter instructs elders to use oversight

1 Peter 5:5 — Young men are to respect the elders

Additionally, elders as pluralities are mentioned in passing in: Acts 11:30; 14:23; 15:2, 4, 22, 23; 16:4; 20:17; 21:18.

APPENDIX TWO

ELDERS, CARE FOR YOUR PASTOR

Questions for creating a culture of soul-care in your local church:

Care Has Legs

Elders, care for your pastor by providing a constant stream of care flowing from a heart of loving initiative.

> *"The purpose in a man's heart is like deep water, but a man of understanding will draw it out."* — Proverbs 20:5

Care Initiates

- How is your soul?
- Where is the gospel real to you right now?
- Are you connecting well with your wife and kids this week?
- Where are you being tempted?

Care Prays

- Am I praying for my pastor?
- Does my pastor know and feel that his church is truly praying for him?
- Are my prayers informed by his actual struggles because I've cared enough to take the initiative to ask?
- What passages could I send to my pastor that might encourage him?

Care Has Teeth

Elders, care for your pastor by protecting his priorities and advocating for his family.

> *"Now the overseer is to be above reproach, faithful to his wife . . . He must manage his own family well." — 1 Timothy 3:2, 4*

Care Protects

- Who knows the state of your pastor's marriage?
- Who ensures he's getting time off and faithfully resting?
- Who looks into whether he's "getting real" in his relationships?
- Who asks about internet use or struggles with marriage and parenting?

Care Advocates

- How can you encourage him in his home life?

- Where can you step in to serve his entire family?
- When could you begin implementing a pastoral sabbatical?
- How can you actively create a culture of support for your pastor and his family?

Care Means Open Hands

Elders, care for your pastor by freeing him to dedicate himself to his God-given gifts.

> *". . . in humility value others above yourselves, not looking to your own interests but each of you to the interests of the others."* — *Philippians 2:3–4*

Care Serves

- What can you take off your pastor's plate?
- How can you help him be more strategic and productive?
- What can you say or do to make your pastor feel like more of a success?
- How can you actively and personally appreciate your pastor today?

APPENDIX THREE

FOUR INDICATORS FOR INSPECTING THE HEALTH OF A PLURALITY

1. Agreement: Do We Agree with Each Other?

- Is the doctrinal basis of our unity as a team well-defined?
- Do we have a statement of faith, and if so, do we all affirm our statement of faith?
- Are we growing together theologically through study and discussion?
- Is it clear to me that you have worked hard to understand my positions and can represent them without exaggeration or misrepresentation?
- Is dissent sufficiently principled and coming from a heart that honestly believes this decision may contradict our values or harm the church?
- Will you wisely represent the position of the plurality to others, whether you agree or disagree?

2. Trust: Do We Trust One Another?

- Will you be loyal to God's Word by being completely honest with me?
- Will you judge me or exploit me when I show weakness?
- Will you be patient with me in areas I need to grow?
- Can you be discreet once you really know my temptations?
- Am I confident that you will not share what I confide with anyone who should not know?
- Do you have my back?
- Will you be humble if I risk correcting you?

3. Care: Do We Care for Each Other?

- Is it clear to each of us that our state of soul matters to each other as much as (or more than!) our performance?
- Are conversations more likely to encourage or critique?
- Can we point out specific times where we talk about our lives, families, struggles and/or temptations (something apart from ministry!)?
- Does my feedback on your performance include encouragement?
- Does someone on this team know where I am vulnerable to temptation?
- Would my wife feel free to call you if I was tanking? Why or why not?

4. Fit: Do We Enjoy Each Other and Know Where We Fit?

- Does my personality appear to mesh with these men?
- Are we able to work together in ways that deepen our relationships rather than strain them?
- Do I know my role and what is expected of me?
- Have we clearly defined how we will evaluate one another and what determines success?
- Am I aware of the specific and regular contexts where we will evaluate our fruitfulness as a team?

ACKNOWLEDGMENTS

The word "acknowledgement" hardly does justice to the gratitude I feel to the folks who helped in this project. It seems almost trite when I set these words alongside of the thanks I truly feel.

So for the moment, assume "acknowledgements" means "stupendously thankful" and let the gratitude begin with Casey Smith and Matt Johnson, the team assembled to edit and produce this project. A special thanks to our managing editor, Justin Karl, who applied his many talents to this project, and this entire series, to ensure pastors and leaders had more practical tools for ministry. Well-done Justin! Finally, to Kimm, the kids and grandkids — for their undeserved enthusiasm for my writing efforts and unending love for me.

ABOUT THE AUTHOR

Dave Harvey serves as the Executive Director of Sojourn Network and a Teaching Pastor at Summit Church in Naples, Florida. Dave is also the founder of *Am I Called.com*, a leadership resource site helping pastors, leaders, and men who sense a call to ministry.

He has 33 years of pastoral experience, with 19 years as a lead pastor. Dave chairs the board for the Christian Counseling and Educational Foundation (CCEF) and has traveled nationally and internationally doing conferences where he teaches Christians, equips pastors, and trains church planters.

Dave has a D.Min from Westminster Theological Seminary, writes regularly for *The Gospel Coalition*, *For The Church*, and is the author of *When Sinners Say I Do*, *Am I Called*, *Rescuing Ambition*, and *Letting Go: Rugged Love for Wayward Souls*. Married for 36 years, Dave and Kimm have four kids and two grandkids.

ABOUT SOJOURN NETWORK

Throughout the pages of the New Testament, and especially in the book of Acts, we observe a pattern: men and women, through prayer and dependence of God and empowered by the Spirit, are sent by God (often through suffering) to spread the Word of the Lord. As this great news of new life in Christ spread into the neighboring cities, regions, provinces, and countries, gatherings of new believers formed into local communities called churches. As these gatherings formed by the thousands in the first century, the early church – taking its cue from the Scriptures — raised up qualified, called, and competent men to lead and shepherd these new congregations.

Two-thousand years later, God is still multiplying his gospel in and through his church, and the Good Shepherd is still using pastors to lead and shepherd God's people. In Sojourn Network, we desire to play our part in helping these pastors plant, grow, and multiply healthy churches.

We realize that only the Spirit can stir people's hearts and bring them into community with other believers in Jesus. Yet, by offering the pastors in our network a strong vision of planting, growing, and multiplying healthy churches and by providing them with thorough leadership assessment, funding for new churches and staff, coaching, training, renewal, and resources, we can best steward their gifts for the benefit and renewal of their local congregations.

Since 2011, our aim at Sojourn Network has been to provide the care and support necessary for our pastors to lead their churches with strength and joy — and to finish ministry well.

OTHER "HOW-TO" BOOKS

Here are the current books in the "How-To" series. Stay tuned for more.

Healthy Plurality = Durable Church: "How-To" Build and Maintain a Healthy Plurality of Elders by Dave Harvey

Life-Giving-Groups: "How-To" Grow Healthy, Multiplying Community Groups by Jeremy Linneman

Before the Lord, Before the Church: "How-To" Plan a Child Dedication Service by Jared Kennedy with Megan Kennedy

Filling Blank Spaces: "How-To" Work with Visual Artists in Your Church by Michael Winters

Redemptive Participation: A "How-To" Guide for Pastors in Culture by Mike Cosper

Charting the Course: "How-To" Navigate the Legal Side of a Church Plant by Tim Beltz

Leaders at Every Level: "How-To" Develop Leaders in the Local Church by Kevin Galloway (forthcoming)

Life-Giving-Groups: "How-To" Grow Healthy, Multiplying Community Groups by Jeremy Linneman

After many years of leading small groups and coaching hundreds of small group leaders, pastor and writer Jeremy Linneman has come to a bold conviction: Community groups are the best place for us — as relational beings — to become mature followers of Christ. This short book seeks to answer two questions: How can our community groups cultivate mature disciples of Christ? And how can our groups grow and multiply to sustain a healthy church? Whether you are new to community groups or tired from years of challenging ministry, *Life-Giving Groups* is a fresh, practical invitation to life together in Christ.

Before the Lord, Before the Church: "How-To" Plan a Child Dedication Service by Jared Kennedy with Megan Kennedy

Is child dedication just a sentimental moment to celebrate family with "oohs and ahhs" over the babies? Or is it a solemn moment before God and a covenanting one before the local church? Kennedy explains a philosophy of child dedication with poignant "How-To" plan for living out a powerful witness to Christ for one another and before the watching world. Whether you are rescuing various forms of child dedication from sentimentalism or perhaps sacrament, this book will guide you to faithful and fruitful ministry honoring God for the gift of children while blessing your church.

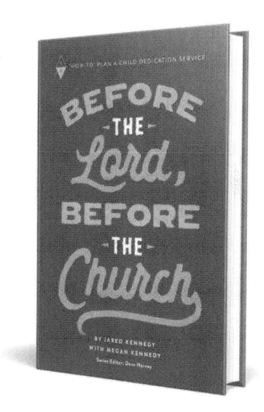

Filling Blank Spaces: "How-To" Work with Visual Artists in Your Church by Michael Winters

"For the relationship between artists and church leaders to flourish, there is a need for wise diplomats who understand both communities and, even better, who love both communities. They also need to know what they are talking about. They need clear-headed ideas and a concrete sense of the practical dimension of this joint work. This is what we have in Michael Winters' book, *Filling Blank Spaces*. Michael is a winsome, generous-spirited mediator who has produced an excellent resource that will no doubt be helpful to many church communities."

David Taylor, Assistant Professor of Theology and Culture, Fuller Theological Seminary, and Director of Brehm Texas

91500175R00064

Made in the USA
Lexington, KY
22 June 2018